THE ANCIENT ROMANS

6

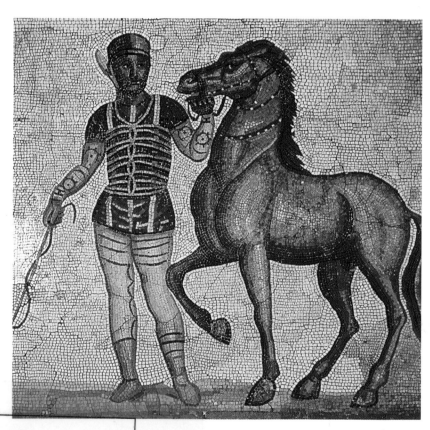

ANITA GANERI

an imp

D0259054

HISTORY STARTS HERE!
The Ancient Romans

OTHER TITLES IN THE SERIES
The Ancient Egyptians • The Ancient Greeks
• The Tudors •

Produced for Wayland Publishers Limited by
Roger Coote Publishing
Gissing's Farm
Fressingfield
Suffolk IP21 5SH
England

Designer: Victoria Webb
Editor: Alex Edmonds
Illustrations: Michael Posen
Cover artwork: Kasia Posen

First published in Great Britain in 1999
by Wayland Publishers Ltd
Reprinted in 2000 by Hodder Wayland,
an imprint of Hodder Children's Books
© Hodder Wayland 1999
This paperback edition published in 2003

Hodder Children's Books,
a division of Hodder Headline Limited
338 Euston Road, London NW1 3BH

British Library Cataloguing in Publication Data
Ganeri, Anita
  The Ancient Romans. – (History starts here)
  1. Rome – History – Empire, 30 bc–476 ad – Juvenile literature
  2. Rome – Civilization – Juvenile literature
  I. Title
  937'.06

ISBN 0 7502 4450 X

Printed and bound in Italy
by G. Canale & C.S.p.A., Turin

Front cover picture: A wall painting from Pompeii showing a man and wife.
Title page picture: A mosaic showing a charioteer in Rome.

Picture acknowledgements:
CM Dixon: front cover, 1, 4, 6, 10, 11, 13, 14, 15, 17, 21, 22, 27, 29; ET Archive:
19, 23, 25; Fishbourne Roman Palace: 18; Tony Stone Images: 7 (Stephen Studd),
9 (Jean Pragen), 20 (Robert Frerck), 28 (Adrian Neal); Werner Forman Archive: 12, 26.

CONTENTS

WHO WERE THE ROMANS?

A famous story tells how Rome was built by two brothers called Romulus and Remus. But the brothers quarrelled and Remus was killed. Romulus became the first king of Rome.

This statue shows Romulus and Remus and a wolf. As babies, the brothers were left by the river to die. But the wolf found them and looked after them.

At the height of their power, the Romans ruled over a huge empire. The green shading shows the Roman Empire in about AD 117.

Today Rome is a busy city full of traffic and crowds. But early Rome was very different. The first Romans lived in a few hillside villages along the River Tiber.

Over hundreds of years, the villages grew into a great and powerful city. By about 2,000 years ago, Rome ruled over the whole of Italy and many other countries besides. These became known as the Roman Empire.

BUILDING AN EMPIRE

The Roman emperor was the most powerful Roman of all. He ruled Rome with the help of the Senate. This was a group of officials who were in charge of the army, taxes and law and order.

The empire ruled over many different countries. At first, some of them tried to fight against Roman rule. But they gradually accepted being part of the empire.

AUGUSTUS

The first Roman emperor was Augustus. He ruled from 27 BC to AD 14. Augustus was a wise and fair ruler who made Rome very peaceful and wealthy. After his death, he was made a god.

The Romans liked to put up statues of the emperors and gods in market places and city squares. This is a statue of Augustus.

The forum was a square in the city centre. It was used as a market and meeting place for friends. Around it were government buildings and temples. These are the ruins of the forum in Rome.

THE CITY OF ROME

Rome was the biggest city in the empire, with about a million people living there. The city was busy, noisy and full of hustle and bustle as people went to work, did the shopping or went to the baths for a massage and sauna.

Roman streets were narrow and crowded. No transport was allowed through them during the day.

Many buildings in Rome were paid for by the emperor to show off his wealth. They included grand temples, halls and arches.

The Colosseum in Rome was a huge amphitheatre where people went to watch gladiator fights. There was room for 50,000 people. You can still visit its ruins today.

RICH AND POOR

In Rome, people were divided into groups based on their family backgrounds, jobs and wealth. Citizens could vote in elections and join the army. At first, you only counted as a citizen if you had Roman parents. Later, other people were allowed to be citizens.

The richest citizens were called patricians. They held important government posts. Then came the equites or merchants. Ordinary citizens were called plebeians.

The richest Romans had grand houses in the country. They were called villas. This luxurious villa was built for Emperor Hadrian on a clifftop outside Rome.

Wealthy families had slaves to do the cooking, shopping and other household tasks.

All the hardest, dirtiest jobs were done by slaves. They were often prisoners of war brought to Rome to be sold at market. Slaves had no rights or freedom.

LIFE IN A ROMAN TOWN

Life in Roman times was very different if you were rich or poor. Poorer Romans lived in cramped blocks of flats with shops and taverns on the ground floor. The flats had no kitchens or running water. People ate take-away food and fetched water from a fountain.

Roman blocks of flats were badly built and often burned down.

Wealthy Romans built their houses around airy courtyards and gardens. This beautiful house in the Roman town of Pompeii belonged to the Vettii family.

Wealthy Romans had comfortable lives. In town, they lived in large, private houses, decorated with statues and mosaics. Many houses had their own water supply and central heating. In summer, the family moved to their country estate to escape from the heat and crowds.

GOING TO SCHOOL

Many Roman children did not go to school. They went out to work. Children from wealthier families started school at the age of six or seven. They were taught how to read, write and do sums. Later, they learned poetry, history and public speaking. The Romans spoke Latin.

Like children today, Roman boys and girls played with toys such as marbles, dolls and toy animals. They also raced toy chariots.

Children learned to write by scratching their letters on to a wax board. They used pointed sticks as pens.

This picture shows a Roman girl thinking about what to write. Most Roman girls did not go to school. They stayed at home and helped their mothers.

ROMAN ROBES

Most Romans wore clothes made from wool or linen. Only wealthy Romans could afford costly cotton and silk. For working and sleeping in, men wore simple tunics. Important men wore long white robes called togas. Women wore tunics with a long dress on top.

CHILDREN'S CLOTHES

Most children wore tunics. Some boys wore togas with a thin purple stripe. When they were 14, there was a special ceremony and the boy was given a plain white toga to wear. He was then seen as a grown up.

You could tell a Roman's place in society by his clothes. A senator's toga was decorated with a purple stripe. Only the richest people could afford the purple dye.

This Roman sandal was found in Britain. It had leather laces to tie it on.

Men and women wore open leather sandals. In parts of the empire where the weather was cold, people wore boots.

Wealthy women liked make-up and jewellery, and had slaves to help them style their hair. Many women wore wigs. Most men had short hair and were clean-shaven.

FOOD AND DRINK

In wealthy families, the kitchen was well equipped with pots, pans, and pottery jars for storing oil and wine. Bread was baked in a stone oven. The cooking was done by slaves.

The Romans usually ate three meals a day. For breakfast, they had bread and fruit. Lunch was a light snack of bread with leftover vegetables.

Dinner was the main meal of the day. It was eaten in the late afternoon. Most people drank water or wine, mixed with water.

Poor people ate simple food. But richer families gave dinner parties where guests ate delicacies such as stuffed dormouse, or flamingo in spicy sauce. The diners did not sit on chairs. They lay on couches around the table.

This mosaic shows a Roman feast.

GODS AND TEMPLES

The Romans worshipped many different gods and goddesses. Their chief god was Jupiter who ruled the sky and was god of thunder and lightning. The Romans built many temples to the gods. They believed the temples were the gods' homes on earth.

Every Roman home had its own small shrine where the family worshipped every day. They prayed to special household gods to look after their home and family. Sometimes they left food and wine for the gods.

The Romans also worshipped the emperor as a god. These are the ruins of a temple dedicated to Emperor Trajan.

Each temple had a statue of its god or goddess. This is Minerva, the Roman goddess of war, wisdom and handicrafts. She was often shown wearing armour like a soldier.

FUN AND GAMES

After a hard morning's work, many Romans set off for the public baths. Here they bathed in hot and cold pools and exercised in the gymnasium. Then it was time for a snack or a massage. Roman baths were great meeting places where people went to relax with their friends.

These are the ruins of the Roman baths at Bath, England. The baths were built over a hot spring which bubbled up from the rocks. Bathers thought this water was good for their health.

This mosaic shows an actor in a play, beating a tambourine. Music was very important in Roman life. It was also played at gladiator fights, festivals, weddings and funerals.

On public holidays, the Romans flocked to watch the chariot racing. Everyone cheered on their favourite team. The races were fast and furious. Many charioteers were killed. Gladiator fights were also very popular. Armed only with nets, spears, small shields or swords, the gladiators often fought to the death.

IN THE ARMY

The Roman army was the best and strongest in the world. It conquered many new countries, guarded the empire's borders and helped to keep the peace. Soldiers joined up for 20 to 25 years.

Ordinary soldiers were called legionaries. They had to be tough to survive. In between fighting, soldiers had to march long distances with heavy packs on their backs. When they stopped at night, they set up camp, and then moved on in the morning.

A Roman legionary wore a woollen tunic, with a metal breast plate and helmet. In cold places, soldiers also wore thick cloaks. They were armed with a short sword, a javelin and a shield.

In peacetime, soldiers helped build roads and forts across the empire. This carving comes from a huge column in Rome, built by Emperor Trajan. It shows many scenes from army life.

TRAVEL AND TRADE

Roman soldiers built thousands of kilometres of roads. These were mainly used for moving soldiers around the empire. Roman roads took the shortest, straightest path between two places. They were so well made, you can still see some of them today.

The Via Appia was the first main Roman road. It ran south from Rome to the town of Capua. This is what the road looks like today.

This is a merchant ship arriving at Ostia. Ships brought wheat from Egypt, cotton from India and wild animals from Africa.

The roads were also important for trade. Other goods were carried by sea. Every day, the port of Ostia near Rome was busy with ships loading and unloading their cargoes.

27

THE END OF THE EMPIRE

28

HOW DO WE KNOW?

We know a lot about the Romans because they left so many things behind. There are many ruins of Roman buildings. We use many Latin words when we speak. Objects such as pots, toys, clothes and jewellery help us to find out about Roman life.

In the third century AD, the Roman empire began to break up. The emperors fought each other and people were unhappy at rising prices and taxes. Emperor Diocletian split the empire into two.

Rome was destroyed by people called the Goths 200 years later. But the other half of the empire lasted for much longer. It finally fell in AD 1453.

Constantine the Great ruled the Eastern Roman empire until he conquered the West in AD 312. He was the first Christian emperor. He built churches around Rome and encouraged the Roman people to become Christians.

The Romans were skilled engineers and builders. They built this aqueduct in France in 16 BC. It is still standing today.

29

IMPORTANT DATES

c. 753 BC Rome was built by two brothers, called Romulus and Remus, according to an ancient legend. Romulus became the first king of Rome.

c. 600 BC The Latin language was first written down.

c. 510 BC The last king of Rome was overthrown. Rome became a republic. This means a country without a king, queen or emperor.

264–146 BC The Romans fought three wars against the powerful city of Carthage in North Africa. In the second war, the great general Hannibal crossed the Alps on elephant back to attack the Romans. The Romans were victorious.

59 BC Julius Caesar became one of the leaders of Rome.

44 BC Julius Caesar was murdered because he was becoming too powerful.

27 BC Augustus became the first emperor of Rome. Rome was now called an empire.

AD 14 Augustus died. His stepson, Tiberius, became emperor.

14–37 Tiberius ruled Rome.

37–41 Caligula ruled Rome. He went mad and was murdered.

42–54 Claudius ruled Rome. His armies began the Roman conquest of Britain.

54–68 Nero ruled Rome.

64 A terrible fire destroyed Rome. Emperor Nero was said to have started it deliberately.

69 Four emperors took turns in ruling. One of them, Vespasian, seized power.

69–79 Vespasian ruled Rome.

79–81 Titus ruled Rome.

80 The Colosseum was opened in Rome by Emperor Titus.

81–96 Domitian ruled.

96–98 Nerva ruled.

98–117 Trajan ruled. The empire reached its largest size. Trajan built his famous column in Rome to celebrate his battle victories.

117–138 Hadrian ruled. He built huge walls at the borders of the empire. One of these was Hadrian's Wall in northern Britain.

284–285 Emperor Diocletian divided the empire into east and west. He ruled the east.

312–337 Constantine ruled. He built a new city in the east, called Constantinople.

410 Rome was raided by the Goths.

455 Rome was raided again, and destroyed.

476 The last emperor of the west was overthrown and the western empire collapsed. The eastern empire lasted until 1453. It was called the Byzantine Empire.

GLOSSARY

Amphitheatre A huge round building where the Romans went to watch fights between gladiators and wild beast shows.

Aqueduct A type of bridge built to carry water from one side of a valley to the other.

Cargoes Goods carried by ship and today, by lorries and aircraft.

Clean-shaven This means not having a moustache or beard.

Elections Contests where people vote for the best person for a job.

Empire A group of countries ruled over by an emperor.

Javelins Long, pointed spears used by Roman soldiers.

Linen A type of cloth made from the flax plant.

Marble A hard shiny stone which is used to make buildings or statues.

Mosaics Patterns of tiny coloured tiles which were used to decorate Roman walls and floors. The tiles were pressed into wet plaster. Making a mosaic was very skilful work.

Senate The officials who ruled Rome. At first, they ruled on their own. Later they had to obey the emperor.

Senator A member of the Senate.

FURTHER INFORMATION

BOOKS TO READ

The Roman Empire by Nigel Kelly, Rosemary Rees and Jane Shuter (Heinemann Living through History series, 1997)

Step into the Roman Empire by Philip Steele (Lorenz Books, 1997)

Emperors and Gladiators by Anita Ganeri (Heinemann All in a Day's Work series, 1997)

The Romans by Anita Ganeri (Watts Focus On series, 2001)

Roman Palace by Tim Wood (A&C Black What Happened Here? series, 2000)

How Would You Survive as an Ancient Roman? by Anita Ganeri (Watts, 1999)

You Wouldn't Want To Be a Roman Gladiator by John Malam (Hodder Wayland, 2001)

INDEX